Bride of Christ
A 40 Day Journey

PRESS

Foreword

This 40 day journey is to be an encouragement to the Bride of Christ. Often times we get engrossed in our daily responsibilities and lose sight of our general purpose. As believers, we're supposed to be the change the world so desperately seeks. In their heart of hearts they know the truth, but there's nothing like seeing the difference His presence can make. I live in Missouri - the show me state. I've come to realize the attitude, belief, actions and faith of one person can impact a multitude. Together we can reclaim the earth for Jesus. Accordingly, each of us has a role in destiny. Are you willing to accept your assigned commission?

God began preparing me for our trip to Israel in early 2009. My friend Rosemary told me of an intercessory prayer course being taught at our church (Destiny Church) by Kent Henry. Needless to say, the depth of worship was significant and the encounters with God numerous. Often times I would receive a vision and a corresponding scripture or word of encouragement. This 'process' continued up to, during and following the trip. Many of the visions I received before the trip were seen in physical form while on the trip. For instance, I saw a tree with one of its roots in a river - a flower blossom was growing from the top of this root. My husband, Bob and I determined to brave the frigid water of the Jordan River in order to receive the blessing of a forward baptism. Curt Landry then asked for 12 volunteers to swim across the river as a representation of the 12 tribes. On the other side was a tree with a root in the water with a flower blossom. I had a chill upon seeing this confirmation and it wasn't because of the water temperature.

While I may have been given a glimpse of what the trip had in store for me personally, nothing could have prepared me for the miracles we saw unfold before our very eyes. My husband is a Vietnam veteran with three Purple Heart accommodations. He has battled with his emotional scars for decades. As a visual person, he has not been able to divorce himself from what he endured while in Vietnam. On the 4th day of our journey, the itinerary was modified - we were now going to St. Ann's Church. The acoustics were phenomenal. We waited patiently while the group before us sung their song of worship. Bob had determined to remain outside. As we began to sing Hallelujah, he knew he was supposed to be with us. Simultaneously we learned we had inadvertently cut in front of another group - they were supposed to sing next. As this was being sorted, Curt Landry was trying to locate Bob as he was entering the church - upon arriving at the altar, it was determined that the church was from Vietnam. Bob was able to express his love for the Vietnamese people, pray for a woman who we think lost her son during the conflict and in turn, receive both emotional and spiritual healing. No one could have orchestrated this string of events except our Creator. Low and behold, St. Ann's is located next to the pool of Bethesda.

When we returned to St. Louis, I felt inclined to commit this journal to paper. I was encouraged to learn it was to be a 40 day devotion to help prepare His Bride for His return. I hope you're able to apply longstanding truths to your daily life and remain forever changed.

All of the pictures at the bottom of each page were taken in Israel in November 2009. The other pictures were taken during our various travels over the years. We hope you embrace your personal journey.

Jodi Gay

Day 1 Pause

Do you see Me?

Through all the noise, all the distractions My hand <u>is</u> at work.

Slow down to see.

Deuteronomy 1:6-8 ... You have stayed long enough at this mountain. Break camp and advance into the hill country ... go to all the neighboring peoples ... in the mountains, in the western foothills ... and along the coast ... as far as the great river ... See, I have given you this land. Go in and <u>take possession</u> of the land that the Lord swore he would give to your fathers – to Abraham, Isaac and Jacob – and to their descendants after them. (emphasis added)

1:18 ... at that time I told you everything you were to do.

You know you hear from Me. Now what are you going to do?

Personal Revelations;

Our journey started at the lowest point on earth, in the desert adjacent to the Dead Sea

Day 2 Play your part

Humble

Will you be My hands?

We must be one – so you can move with unwavering confidence – particularly when all physical evidence is contrary to what you know to be true in the Spirit.

Go into all nations

Plant seeds

See immediate change

Stand (as watchmen on the wall) in the place you've been planted.

Isaiah 62:6-7 ... never be silent day or night. You who call on the Lord, give yourselves no rest, and give Him no rest till He establishes Jerusalem and makes her the praise of the earth.

Build My people.

Malachi 3:16 ... a scroll of remembrance was written in His presence concerning those who feared the Lord and honored His name.

Personal Revelations;

Landscaping dental clinic, Sderot

Day 3 Life

Your current state is not your fate – there is life in the desert.

2 Corinthians 6:2 ... <u>now</u> is the time of God's favor (emphasis added)

Faith

-calls the things that are not as though they were

-brings into being what God has already appropriated by grace

-is the voice that speaks tomorrow's realities into today

-is the voice that silences the echo chambers of our past. God does not hear your echoes; He hears your voice. (Curt Landry)

Cut away the iniquity that limits. Where there is water, there <u>is</u> life.

Personal Revelations;

Day 4   Tranquility

Psalm 23:1-4 The Lord is my shepherd. I shall not be in want. He makes me lie down in green pastures, He leads me beside quiet waters, He restores my soul. He guides me in paths of righteousness for His name's sake. Even though I walk through the valley of the shadow of death, I will fear no evil, for You <u>are</u> with me. (emphasis added)

Once you have heard -->→ say. Then, you have to obey. To speak is more important than to see. You'll be blessed from glory to glory.

Personal Revelations;

Day 5 Perseverance

Psalm 1:1-3 Blessed is the man ... his delight is in the law of the Lord, and on His law he meditates day and night. He is like a tree planted by streams of water, which yields its fruit in season and whose leaf does not wither. Whatever he does prospers.

Jeremiah 17:7-8 Blessed is the man who trusts in the Lord, whose confidence is in Him. He will be like a tree planted by the water that sends out its roots by the stream. It does not fear when heat comes; its leaves are always green. It has no worries in a year of drought and <u>never</u> fails to bear fruit. (emphasis added)

Jeremiah 12:5 If you have raced with men on foot and they have worn you out, how can you compete with the horses? If you stumble in safe country, how will you manage in the thickets by the Jordan?

How will you endure even greater injustices?

Personal Revelations;

Revelation 2:7 To him who overcomes,
I will give the right to eat from the tree of life.

Day 6 Look Forward

You will **never** be alone.

Psalm 48:14 For this God is our God forever and ever; he will be our guide even to the end.

Habakkuk 2:1-3 I will stand at my watch and station myself on the ramparts; I will look to see what he will say to me, and what answer I am to give ... Then the Lord replied: Write down the revelation and make it plain on tablets ... For the revelation awaits an appointed time; it speaks of the end and will not prove false. Though it linger, wait for it; it will certainly come and will not delay.

Ezekiel 12:23-25 ... 'The days are near when every vision will be fulfilled. For there will be no more false visions or flattering divinations among the people of Israel. But I the Lord will speak what I will, and it shall be fulfilled without delay.'

Psalm 85:8 I will listen to what God the Lord will say; he promises peace to his people, his saints ...

Personal Revelations;

Forward baptism – Jordan River

Day 7 Unity

Colossians 3:1-17 ... set your hearts on things above ... put on the new self, which is being renewed in knowledge. Here there is no ... circumcised or uncircumcised, but Christ is all, and is in all. Therefore, as God's chosen people, holy and dearly loved, clothe yourself with compassion, kindness, humility, gentleness and patience. Bear with each other and forgive whatever grievances you may have against one another. Forgive as the Lord forgave you. And over all these virtues put on love, which binds them all together in perfect unity. Let the peace of Christ rule in your hearts, since as members of one body you were called to peace. And be thankful. Let the Word of Christ dwell in you richly as you teach and admonish one another with all wisdom, and as you sing psalms, hymns and spiritual songs with gratitude in your hearts to God. And whatever you do, whether in word or deed, do it all in the name of the Lord Jesus, giving thanks to God the Father through Him.

Ephesians 2:14-16 For He Himself is our peace, who has made the two one and has destroyed the barrier, the dividing wall of hostility, by abolishing in His flesh the law with its commandments and regulations. His purpose was to create in Himself one new man out of two, thus making peace, and in this one body to reconcile both of them to God through the cross, by which He put to death their hostility.

Personal Revelations;

Uncommon collaboration: Mayor of Sderot, Messianic Rabbi, Former Israeli Minister of Defense, Orthodox Rabbi; blessing dental clinic with a mezuzzah

Day 8   Courage

Psalm 91:1-16 He who dwells in the shelter of the Most High will rest in the shadow of the Almighty. I will say of the Lord, "He is my refuge and my fortress, my God, in whom I trust." ... For He will command His angels concerning you to guard you in all your ways ... "Because he loves me," says the Lord, "I will rescue him; I will protect him, for he acknowledges My name. He will call upon Me, and I will answer him; I will be with him in trouble, I will deliver him and honor him. With long life will I satisfy him and show him My salvation."

1 Samuel 24:6,12 "The Lord forbid that I should ... lift my hand against ... the anointed of the Lord." May the Lord judge between you and me.

Maintain a pure heart - for where can you go from My Spirit? There is no need to hide. For I know the plans I have for you **Jeremiah 29:11**

John 18:9 ... I have not lost one of those you gave me

Protect My children (people).

Personal Revelations;

Judean desert of En Gedi – where David hid from Saul

School (with reinforced roof), Sderot

Day 9 Obedience

Matthew 26:36-45 Then Jesus went with his disciples to a place called Gethsemane, and He said to them, "Sit here while I go over there and pray." ... "Stay here and keep watch with Me." ... He fell with His face to the ground and prayed, "My Father, if it is possible, may this cup be taken from me. Yet not as I will, but as You will." Then He returned to His disciples and found them sleeping. "Could you men not keep watch with Me for one hour? Watch and pray so that you will not fall into temptation. The Spirit is willing, but the body is weak." He went away a second time and prayed. "My Father, if it is not possible for this cup to be taken away unless I drink it, may Your will be done." When He came back, He again found them sleeping ... "look, the hour is near ..."

Now is <u>not</u> the time to be asleep. <u>Arise</u>.

St. Paul's Pillar, Pafos, Cyprus

Personal Revelations;

Day 10 and 11   Trust

The enemy's attempt to oppress has been real. But My name is above all names. I am alive. I am in control. You can rely upon Me. I will not forsake you. I will protect you. I have endured the same challenges, the same emotions as you - you have to remember, those who believe, who remain steadfast <u>are</u> victorious. You must stand on the truth - on My Word.

Personal Revelations;

"Seven sculptured relief panels reflecting the last seven utterances from the crucifixion ... seven life size bronze figures symbolizing the response and reflection of the Holocaust ... six pillars of stone for a memorial of the six million perished."

'The Fountain of Tears'
A dialogue of suffering between the Holocaust and the Crucifixion by Artist: Rick Wienecke

"Father, forgive them for they know not what they do.

"Today you will be with Me in paradise."

"Mother, this is your son.
" Son, this is your mother."

"My God, My God,
why have you forsaken me?"

"I thirst""

It is complete."

Day 12 Break the Barriers

My hands, your hands. Do you see Me? I desire an intimate relationship with you. Do not ... bow down to the work of (your) hands **Isaiah 2:8** (lit. inclusion) **Let Me mold you and shape you ... so My light will shine through you – for all to see My glory. Freedom come down.**

Psalm 40:1-17 I waited patiently for the Lord; He turned to me and heard my cry. He lifted me out of the slimy pit, out of the mud and mire; He set my feet on a rock and gave me a firm place to stand. He put a new song in my mouth, a hymn of praise to our God. Many will see and fear and put their trust in the Lord. Blessed is the man who makes the Lord his trust, who does not look to the proud, to those who turn aside to false gods. Many, O Lord my God, are the wonders you have done. The things you planned for us no one can recount to you; were I to speak and tell of them, they would be too many to declare. Sacrifice and offering you did not desire, but my ears you have pierced; burnt offerings and sin offerings you did not require. Then I said, here I am, I have come – it is written about me in the scroll. I desire to do your will, O my God; your law is written within my heart. I proclaim righteousness in the great assembly!; I do not seal my lips, as you know, O Lord. I do not hide your righteousness in my heart; I speak of your faithfulness and salvation. I do not conceal your love and your truth from the great assembly. Do not withhold your mercy from me, O Lord; may your love and your truth always protect me. For troubles without number surround me; my sins have overtaken me, and I cannot see. They are more than the hairs on my head, and my heart fails within me. Be pleased, O Lord, to save me; O Lord, come quickly to help me. May all who seek to take my life be put to shame and confusion; may all who desire my ruin be turned back in disgrace. May those who say to me, "Aha! Aha!" be appalled at their own shame. But may all who seek you rejoice and be glad in you; may those who love your salvation always say, "The Lord be exalted!" Yet I am poor and needy; may the Lord think of me. You are my help and my deliverer; O my God, do not delay.

Hosea 6:2 After two days he will revive us; on the third day he will restore us, that we may live in his presence ... let us press on to acknowledge him.

1 Corinthians 13:12 ... then we shall see face to face ... then I shall know fully.

Open the doors – release My presence. My glory results in a change in the environment. Faithfulness shall pierce the darkness. You have authority over the oppression of this world. The enemy will be bound. My will be done on earth as it is in heaven. Now is the time – for I desire that none shall perish. Reach out – pull them to the safety of My wings ... into My kingdom.

Personal Revelations;

"Into your hands I commend My Spirit."

Day 13 Provision

Deuteronomy 8:16-20 He gave you manna to eat in the desert, something your fathers had never known, to humble and to test you so that in the end it might go well with you. You may say to yourself, "My power and the strength of my hands have produced this wealth for me." But remember the Lord your God, for it is He who gives you the ability to produce wealth, and so confirms His covenant, which He swore to your forefathers, as it is today. If you ever forget the Lord your God and follow other gods and worship and bow down to them, I testify against you today that you will surely be destroyed. Like the nations the Lord destroyed before you, so you will be destroyed for not obeying the Lord your God.

Revelation 2:17 He who has an ear, let him hear what the Spirit says to the churches. To him who overcomes, I will give some of the hidden manna.

Personal Revelations;

Dinner in an authentic Bedouin tent

Day 14 Preparation

Proverbs 16:9 … the Lord determines his steps.

Galatians 5:25 Since we live by the Spirit, let us keep in step with the Spirit.

One step at a time

The climb may become steeper

Do not get ahead of Me

Learn to wait (as David did)

Psalm 85:8 I will listen to what God the Lord will say; He promises peace to His people, His saints –

As you climb each mountain

I will guide each step of your feet

There will be no doubt that it is Me

You will not grow weary

You will not give up

You will not question

You will believe

You will trust

You will lead (others)

James 4:10 Humble yourselves before the Lord, and He will lift you up.

Personal Revelations;

Steps to the ancient fortress of Masada

Day 15 Yield

Psalm 85:10-13 Love and faithfulness meet together; righteousness and peace kiss each other. Faithfulness springs forth from the earth, and righteousness looks down from heaven. The Lord will indeed give what is good, and our land will yield its harvest. Righteousness goes before him and prepares the way for His steps.

Ephesians 5:26-27 ... cleansing her by the washing with water through the Word and to present her to Himself as a radiant church without stain or wrinkle or any other blemish, but holy and blameless.

1. **One step in obedience**

2. **Activate living water (fresh Word of revelation)**

3. **Growth in the Word (do not get complacent)**

4. **Strength in Me**

     Immovable – no compromise

     Invincible

     Confident

     Trusting

     Peaceful

     Transparent authentic reflectors of Christ

     Member of My Body (transform your mind to Kingdom thoughts)

Ephesians 2:19-22 Consequently, you are no longer foreigners and aliens, but fellow citizens with God's people and members of God's household, built on the foundation of the apostles and prophets, with Christ Jesus himself as the chief cornerstone. In Him, the whole building is joined together and rises to become a holy temple in the Lord. And in Him you too are being built together to become a dwelling in which God lives by His Spirit.

Personal Revelations;

Roman theatre at Beth Shean

Day 16 Focus

Matthew 6:19-21 Do not store up for yourselves treasures on earth, where moth and rust destroy, and where thieves break in and steal. But store up for yourselves treasures in heaven, where moth and rust do not destroy, and where thieves do not break in and steal. For where your treasure is, there your heart will be also.

What legacy will you leave behind?

Joshua 1:2-9 "... get ready to cross the Jordan River into the land I am about to give ... I will give you every place where you set your foot ... No one will be able to stand up against you all the days of your life. As I was with Moses, so I will be with you; I will never leave you nor forsake you. Be strong and courageous, because you will lead these people to inherit the land I swore to their forefathers to give them ... Do not be terrified; do not be discouraged, for the Lord your God will be with you wherever you go."

2 Chronicles 7:13-15 "When I shut up the heavens so that there is no rain, or command locusts to devour the land or send a plague among my people, if my people, who are called by my name, will humble themselves and pray and seek my face and turn from their wicked ways, then will I hear from heaven and will forgive their sin and heal their land. Now my eyes will be open and my ears attentive to the prayers offered in this place."

Amos 9:11-12 "In the day I will restore David's fallen tent. I will repair its broken places, restore its ruins, and build it as it used to be, so that they may possess the remnant ..."

Lead with faith and authority.

Personal Revelations;

Remnant of Masada

Day 17 Believe

Witness; proclaim what is to come

Lazarus' Tomb, Larnaka, Cyprus

Ezekiel 47:1-12 The man brought me back to the entrance of the temple, and I saw water coming out from under the threshold of the temple toward the east (for the temple faced east). The water was coming down from under the south side of the temple, south of the altar. He then brought me out through the north gate and led me around the outside to the outer gate facing east, and the water was flowing from the south side. As the man went eastward with a measuring line in his hand, he measured off a thousand cubits and then led me through water that was ankle-deep. He measured off another thousand cubits and led me through water that was knee-deep. He measured off another thousand and led me through water that was up to the waist. He measured off another thousand, but now it was a river that I could not cross, because the water had risen and was deep enough to swim in – a river that no one could cross. He asked me, "Son of man, do you see this?" Then he led me back to the bank of the river. When I arrived there, I saw a great number of trees on each side of the river. He said to me, "This water flows toward the eastern region and goes down into the Arabah, where it enters the Sea. When it empties into the Sea, the water there becomes fresh. Swarms of living creatures will live wherever the river flows. There will be large numbers of fish, because this water flows there and makes the salt water fresh; so where the river flows everything will live. Fishermen will stand along the shore; from En Gedi to En Eglaim there will be places for spreading nets. The fish will be of many kinds – like the fish of the Great Sea. But for the swamps and marshes will not become fresh; they will be left for salt. Fruit trees of all kinds will grow on both banks of the river. Their leaves will not wither, nor will their fruit fail. Every month they will bear, because the water from the sanctuary flows to them. Their fruit will serve for food and their leaves for healing.
1 Corinthians 3:16-17 Don't you know that you yourselves are God's temple and that God's spirit lives in you? If anyone destroys God's temple, God will destroy him; for God's temple is sacred, and you are that temple.

Personal Revelations;

Dead Sea is receding and being replaced with fresh water filled with fish.

Day 18 and 19 Transformation

Philippians 2:5 Your attitude should be the same as that of Christ Jesus.

Colossians 1:9-12 ... asking God to fill you with the knowledge of His will through all spiritual wisdom and understanding ... that you may live a life worthy of the Lord and may please Him in every way: bearing fruit in every good work, growing in the knowledge of God, being strengthened with all power according to His glorious might so that you may have great endurance and patience, and joyfully giving thanks to the Father, who has qualified you to share in the inheritance of the saints in the kingdom of light.

2 Thessalonians 2:1-2 ... we ask you ... not to become easily unsettled or alarmed ...

John 6:63 The Spirit gives life; the flesh counts for nothing. The words I have spoken to you are Spirit and they are life.

2 Corinthians 6:2 ... "In the time of my favor I heard you, and in the day of salvation I helped you. I tell you, now is the time of God's favor, now is the day of salvation."

Personal Revelations;

Eastern Wall (Mercy or Golden Gate)

Western (wailing) Wall

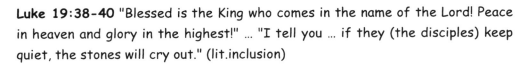

Luke 19:38-40 "Blessed is the King who comes in the name of the Lord! Peace in heaven and glory in the highest!" ... "I tell you ... if they (the disciples) keep quiet, the stones will cry out." (lit.inclusion)

Romans 12:2 Do not conform any longer to the pattern of this world, but be transformed by the renewing of your mind.

Seek Me. Will you allow Me to impart My mind to you?

Southern Steps

Excavation beneath the existing surface

Current day disciples sitting on ancient temple rocks

Day 20 Serve

Isaiah 22:9-11 you saw that the City of David had many breaches in its defenses; you stored up water in the Lower Pool. You counted the buildings in Jerusalem and tore down houses to strengthen the wall. You built a reservoir between the two walls for the water of the Old Pool, but you did not look to the One who made it, or have regard for the One who planned it long ago.

Zechariah 2:4-5 ... 'Jerusalem will be a city without walls because of the great number of men and livestock in it. And I myself will be a wall of fire around it,' declares the Lord, 'and I will be its glory within.'

Have no intent for self protection ... for I planned this long ago. Stand strong at the appointed time. I will give revelation and knowledge. My timing is perfect. My eye will guide.

Zechariah 4:11-14 Then I asked the angel, "What are these two olive trees on the right and the left of the lamp stand?" Again I asked him, "What are these two olive branches beside the two gold pipes that pour out golden oil?" He replied, "Do you not know what these are?" "No, my Lord," I said. So He said, "These are the two who are anointed to serve the Lord of all the earth."

Genesis 15:7-18 ..."I am the Lord, who brought you out ... to give you this land to take possession of it." But Abram said, "O Sovereign Lord, how can I know that I will gain possession of it?" ... on that day the Lord made a covenant with Abram and said, "To your descendants I give this land ..."

Claim the land ... take possession. Your life is as significant as Abraham's, Isaac's and Jacob's ... will you answer the call? Jesus paved the road you're walking.

Personal Revelations;

Day 21 Hope

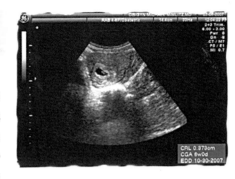

Romans 5:1-5 Therefore, since we have been justified through faith, we have peace with God through our Lord Jesus Christ, through whom we have gained access by faith into this grace in which we now stand. And we rejoice in the hope of the glory of God. Not only so, but we also rejoice in our sufferings, because we know that suffering produces perseverance; perseverance, character; and character, hope. And hope does not disappoint us, because God has poured out His love into our hearts by the Holy Spirit, whom He has given us.

1 Corinthians 15:22-27 For as in Adam all die, so in Christ all will be made alive. But each in his own turn: Christ, the first fruits; then, when He comes, those who belong to Him. Then the end will come, when He hands over the kingdom to God the Father after He has destroyed all dominion, authority and power. For He must reign until He has put all His enemies under His feet. The last enemy to be destroyed is death. For He has put everything under His feet.

1 Thessalonians 4:13-16 Brothers, we do not want you to be ignorant about those who fall asleep, or to grieve like the rest of men, who have no hope. We believe that Jesus died and rose again and so we believe that God will bring with Jesus those who have fallen asleep in him. According to the Lord's own Word, we tell you that we who are still alive, who are left till the coming of the Lord, will certainly not precede those who have fallen asleep. For the Lord himself will come down from heaven, with a loud command, with the voice of the archangel and with the trumpet call of God, and the dead in Christ will rise first.

Life shall rise up regardless of the attempts of the enemy to destroy. Do not be deceived by the lies of the enemy.

John 18:4 ... "Who is it you want?"
I am seeking Him in the blood.

Personal Revelations;

Sun rising over Jerusalem

Day 22   Authority

Psalm 149:1-9 Praise the Lord. Sing to the Lord a new song, his praise in the assembly of the saints. Let Israel rejoice in their Maker; let the people of Zion be glad in their King. Let them praise His name with dancing and make music to Him with tambourine and harp. For the Lord takes delight in His people; He crowns the humble with salvation. Let the saints rejoice in this honor and sing for joy on their beds. May the praise of God be in their mouths and a double-edged sword in their hands, to inflict vengeance on the nations and punishment on the peoples, to bind their kings with fetters, their nobles with shackles of iron, to carry out the sentence written against them. This is the glory of all His saints. Praise the Lord.

Romans 13:1 ...for there is not authority except that which God has established.

2 Corinthians 10:3-5 For though we live in the world, we do not wage war as the world does. The weapons we fight with are not the weapons of the world. On the contrary, they have divine power to demolish strongholds. We demolish arguments and every pretension that sets itself up against the knowledge of God, and we take captive every thought to make it obedient to Christ.

Ephesians 6:10-18 Finally, be strong in the Lord and in His mighty power. Put on the full armor of God so that you can take your stand against the devil's schemes. For our struggle is not against flesh and blood, but against rulers, against the authorities, against the powers of this dark world and against the spiritual forces of evil in the heavenly realms. Therefore, put on the full armor of God, so that when the day of evil comes, you may be able to stand your ground, and after you have done everything, to stand. Stand firm then, with the belt of truth buckled around your waist, with the breastplate of righteousness in place, and with your feet filled with the readiness that comes from the gospel of peace. In addition to all this, take up the shield of faith, with which you can extinguish all the flaming arrows of the evil one. Take the helmet of salvation and the sword of the Spirit, which is the Word of God. And pray in the Spirit on all occasions with all kinds of prayers and requests. With this in mind, be alert and always keep on praying for all the saints.

You shall sing Me praises. You shall take authority. You shall stand. You shall use the weapons I have given you to pierce the darkness. You shall possess the land. You shall declare My glory among the nations.

Personal Revelations;

Day 23 Forgiveness

Revelation 22:1-6 Then the angel showed me the river of water of life, as clear as crystal, flowing from the throne of God and of the Lamb down the middle of the great street of the city. On each side of the river stood the tree of life, bearing twelve crops of fruit, yielding its fruit every month. And the leaves of the tree are for the healing of the nations. No longer will there be any curse. The throne of God and of the Lamb will be in the city, and his servants will serve Him. They will see His face, and His name will be on their foreheads. There will be no more night. They will not need the light of a lamp or the light of the sun, for the Lord God will give them light. And they will reign forever and ever. The angel said to me, "These words are trust worthy and true. The Lord, the God of the spirits of the prophets, sent His angel to show His servant the things that must soon take place."
Miracles in the midst of you. Healing through you.

John 14:9-12 Jesus answered: "Anyone who has seen Me has seen the Father ... Don't you believe that I am in the Father, and that the Father is in Me? The words I say to you are not just my own. Rather, it is the Father, living in me, who is doing His work. I tell you the truth, anyone who has faith in Me will do what I have been doing. He will do even greater things than these because I am going to the Father."

Personal Revelations;

St. Ann Church (adjacent to the pool of Bethesda (John 5:1))

Day 24 Persecution

Romans 8:28-39 And we know that in all things God works for the good of those who love Him, who have been called according to His purpose. For those God foreknew He also predestined to be conformed to the likeness of His Son, that He might be the firstborn among many brothers. And those He predestined, He also called; those He called, He also justified; those He justified, He also glorified. What, then, shall we say in r esponse to this? If God is for us, who can be against us? He who did not spare His own Son, but gave Him up for us all – how will He not also, along with Him, graciously give us all things? Who will bring any charge against those whom God has chosen? It is God who justifies. Who is he that condemns? Christ Jesus, who died – more than that, who was raised to life – is at the right hand of God and is also interceding for us. Who shall separate us from the love of Christ? Shall trouble or hardship or persecution or famine or nakedness or danger or sword? As it is written: For your sake we face death all day long; we are considered as sheep to be slaughtered. No, in all things we are more than conquerors through Him who loved us. For I am convinced that neither death not life, neither angels nor demons, neither the present nor the future, nor any powers, neither height nor depth, nor anything else in all creation, will be able to separate us from the love of God that is in Christ Jesus our Lord.

James 1:16-18 Don't be deceived … He chose to give us birth through the Word of truth, that we might be a kind of firstfruits …

Personal Revelations;

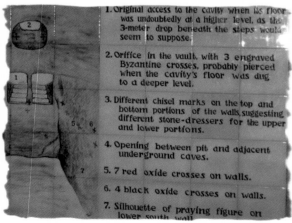

1. Original access to the cavity when its floor was undoubtedly at a higher level, as the 3-meter drop beneath the steps would seem to suppose.

2. Orifice in the vault, with 3 engraved Byzantine crosses, probably pierced when the cavity's floor was dug to a deeper level.

3. Different chisel marks on the top and bottom portions of the walls, suggesting different stone-dressers for the upper and lower portions.

4. Opening between pit and adjacent underground caves.

5. 7 red oxide crosses on walls.

6. 4 black oxide crosses on walls.

7. Silhouette of praying figure on lower south wall.

Day 25 Reverence

Habakkuk 2:20 But the Lord is in His holy temple; let all the earth be silent before Him.

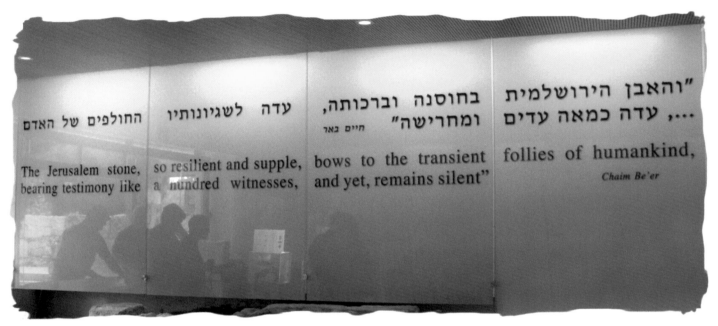

החולפים של האדם   עדה לשגיונותיו   בחוסנה וברכותה,   "והאבן הירושלמית

ומחרישה"   חיים באר   עדה כמאה עדים ,....

The Jerusalem stone, so resilient and supple, bows to the transient follies of humankind, bearing testimony like a hundred witnesses, and yet, remains silent"

Chaim Be'er

Personal Revelations;

Day 26 Peace

Psalm 122:1-9 I rejoiced with those who said to me, "Let us go to the house of the Lord." Our feet are standing in your gates, O Jerusalem. Jerusalem is built like a city that is closely compacted together. That is where the tribes go up, the tribes of the Lord, to praise the name of the Lord according to the statute given to Israel. There the thrones for the statute given to Israel. There the thrones for judgment stand, the thrones of the house of David. Pray for the peace of Jerusalem: "May those who love you be secure. May there be peace within your walls and security within your citadels." For the sake of my brothers and friends, I will say, "Peace be within you." For the sake of the house of the Lord our God, I will seek your prosperity.

Psalm 133:1-3 How good and pleasant it is when brothers live together in unity! It is like precious oil poured on the head, running down on the beard, down upon the collar of his robes. It is as if the dew of Hermon were falling on Mount Zion. For there the Lord bestows His blessing, even life forevermore.

Proverbs 11:30 The fruit of righteousness is a tree of life.

Prophesy onto the wind. Feed My angels the arrows they need. Sow seed – a root in the land of Israel.

Personal Revelations;

Lions Gate

Day 27 Cornerstone

1 Peter 2:4-12 As you come to Him, the living stone – rejected by men but chosen by God and precious to Him – you also, like living stones, are being built into a spiritual house to be a holy priesthood, offering spiritual sacrifices acceptable to God through Jesus Christ. For in scripture it says, "See I lay a stone in Zion, a chosen and precious cornerstone, and the one who trusts in Him will never be put to shame." Now to you who believe, this stone is precious. But to those who do not believe, "The stone the builders rejected has become the capstone," and, "A stone that causes men to stumble and a rock that makes them fall." They stumble because they disobey the message – which is also what they were destined for. But you are a chosen people, a royal priesthood, a holy nation, a people belonging to God, that you may declare the praises of Him who called you out of darkness into His wonderful light. Once you were not a people, but now you are the people of God; once you had not received mercy, but now you have received mercy. Dear friends, I urge you, as aliens and strangers in the world, to abstain from sinful desires, which war against your soul. Live such good lives among the pagans that, though they accuse you of doing wrong, they may see your good deeds and glorify God on the day He visits us.

Isaiah 28:16-17 So this is what the Sovereign Lord says: "See I lay a stone in Zion, a tested stone, a precious cornerstone for a sure foundation; the one who trusts will never be dismayed. I will make justice the measuring line and righteousness the plumb line …

Mark 4:35 … "Let us go over to the other side."

Psalm 23:5-6 You prepare a table before me in the presence of my enemies. You anoint my head with oil; my cup overflows. Surely goodness and love will follow me all the days of my life, and I will dwell in the house of the Lord forever.

I shall pour out the anointing reign

Matthew 4:12-17 When Jesus heard that John had been put in prison, He returned to Galilee. Leaving Nazareth, He went and lived in Capernaum, which was by the lake in the area of Zebulun and Naphtali – to fulfill what was said through the prophet Isaiah: "Land of Zebulun and land of Naphtali, the way to the sea, along the Jordan, Galilee of the Gentiles – the people living in darkness have seen a great light; on those living in the land of the shadow of death a light has dawned." From that time on Jesus began to preach, "Repent, for the kingdom of heaven is near."

Personal Revelations;

Capernaum – center of Jesus' preaching in Galilee

Day 28 Restoration

Matthew 16:17-19 Jesus replied, "Blessed are you, Simon son of Jonah, for this was not revealed to you by man, but by my Father in heaven. And I tell you that you are Peter, and on this rock I will build my church, and the gates of Hades will not overcome it. I will give you the keys of the kingdom of heaven; whatever you bind on earth will be bound in heaven, and whatever you loose on earth will be loosed in heaven."

John 21:15-19 ... "Feed my lambs ... Take care of my sheep ... Feed my sheep ... Follow Me!"

Deuteronomy 28:1-14 If you will fully obey the Lord your God and carefully follow all His commands I give you today, the Lord your God will set you high above all the nations on earth. All these blessings will come upon you and accompany you if you obey the Lord your God: You will be blessed in the city and blessed in the country. The fruit of your womb will be blessed, and the crops of your land and the young of your livestock – the calves of your herds and the lambs of your flocks. Your basket and your kneading trough will be blessed. You will be blessed when you come in and blessed when you go out. The Lord will grant that the enemies who rise up against you will be defeated before you. They will come at you from one direction but flee from you in seven. The Lord will send a blessing on your barns and on everything you put your hand to. The Lord your God will bless you in the land He is giving you. The Lord will establish you as His holy people, as He promised you on oath, if you keep the commands of the Lord your God and walk in His ways. Then all the peoples on earth will see that you are called by the name of the Lord, and they will fear you. The Lord will grant you abundant prosperity – in the fruit of your womb, the young of your livestock and the crops of your ground – in the land he swore to your forefathers to give you. The Lord will open the heavens, the storehouse of His bounty, to send rain on your land in season and to bless all the work of your hands. You will lend to many nations but will borrow from none. The Lord will make you the head, not the tail. If you pay attention to the commands of the Lord your God that I give you this day and carefully follow them, you will always be at the top, never at the bottom. Do not turn aside from any of the commands I give you today, to the right or to the left, following other gods and serving them.

Do not shrink back.

Personal Revelations;

Capernaum - Beach on the shores of Galilee

Day 29 Confidence

Matthew 5:3-10 "Blessed are the poor in spirit, for theirs is the kingdom of heaven. Blessed are those who mourn, for they will be comforted. Blessed are the meek, for they will inherit the earth. Blessed are those who hunger and thirst for righteousness, for they will be filled. Blessed are the merciful, for they will be shown mercy. Blessed are the pure in heart, for they will see God. Blessed are the peacemakers, for they will be called sons of God. Blessed are those who are persecuted because of righteousness, for theirs is the kingdom of heaven."

Do you exhibit the beatitudes when you are challenged?

Hebrews 9:24 For Christ did not enter a man-made sanctuary that was only a copy of a true one; He entered heaven itself, now to appear for us in God's presence.

Hebrews 10:35-39 So do not throw away your confidence; it will be richly rewarded. You need to persevere so that when you have done the will of God, you will receive what He has promised. For in just a very little while, "He who is coming will come and will not delay. But my righteous one will live by faith. And if he shrinks back, I will not be pleased with him." But we are not of those who shrink back and are destroyed, but of those who believe and are saved.

Be ready to save during a storm.

Personal Revelations;

Altar at Capernaum

Day 30 Break Forth

Isaiah 27:6 In days to come Jacob will take root, Israel will bud and blossom and fill all the world with fruit.

Romans 11:16 If the part of the dough offered as first fruits is holy, then the whole batch is holy; if the root is holy, so are the branches.

Zechariah 9:1 The Word of the Lord ... will rest upon Damascus – for the eyes of men and all the tribes of Israel are on the Lord ...

Acts 22:14-16 ...'The God of our fathers has chosen you to know His will and to see the Righteous One and to hear words from His mouth. You will be His witness to all men of what you have seen and heard. And now what you are waiting for? ...'

Connect emotionally with My need, My heart.

<u>Road to Damascus</u>

Could feel My presence when passing through. Soil was prepared in advance. As an evangelical Christian are you going to step up? Break forth the water ... a bountiful garden will prevail.

Personal Revelations;

Minstrel, warring angels appeared
Aroma fell from open heaven.

On the Sea of Galilee

Day 31 Strength

Matthew 6:10 your kingdom come, your will be done on earth as it is in heaven.

Hebrews 11:1-6 Now faith is being sure of what we hope for and certain of what we do not see. This is what the ancients were commended for … without faith it is impossible to please God …

Hebrews 11:33-34 who through faith conquered kingdoms, administered justice, and gained what was promised; … whose weakness was turned to strength; and who became powerful in battle and routed foreign armies.

Personal Revelations;

Caesarea

Day 32 Faith

Can you see the hospital the Lord is going to build?
Canilla, Guatemala

Matthew 5:1-2, 7:15-29 Now when He saw the crowds, He went up on a mountainside and sat down. His disciples came to Him, and He began to teach them, saying: ... "Watch out for false prophets. They come to you in sheep's clothing, but inwardly they are ferocious wolves. By their fruit you will recognize them. Do people pick grapes from thorn bushes, or figs from thistles? Likewise every good tree bears good fruit, but a bad tree bears bad fruit. A good tree cannot bear bad fruit, and a bad tree cannot bear good fruit. Every tree that does not bear good fruit is cut down and thrown into the fire. Thus, by their fruit you will recognize them. Not everyone who says to me, "Lord, Lord,' will enter the kingdom of heaven, but only he who does the will of my Father who is in heaven. Many will say to me on that day, 'Lord, Lord, did we not prophesy in your name, and in your name drive out demons and perform miracles?' Then I will tell them plainly, 'I never knew you. Away from me ...' Therefore everyone who hears these words of mine and puts them into practice is like a wise man who built his house on the rock. The rain came down, the streams rose, and the winds blew and beat against that house; yet it did not fall, because it had its foundation on the rock. But everyone who hears these words of mine and does not put them into practice is like a foolish man who built his house on sand. The rain came down, the streams rose, and the winds blew and beat against that house, and it fell with a great crash." When Jesus had finished saying these things, the crowds were amazed at His teaching, because He taught as one who had authority ...

It's not about you but instead about what you give to the world. Let the Spirit man lead. You will see Me – are you looking? If you are going to be a peacemaker, you must be at peace with yourself.

Personal Revelations;

Mt. Beatitudes – site of the Sermon on the Mount

Day 33   Freedom

1 Kings 18:18 "I have not made trouble for Israel," Elijah replied. "But you and your father's family have. You have abandoned the Lord's commands and have followed the Baals ..."

2 Chronicles 15:2 "... if you forsake Him, He will forsake you."

Psalm 24:1-10 The earth is the Lord's, and everything in it, the world, and all who live in it; for He found it upon the seas and established it upon the waters. Who may ascend the hill of the Lord? Who may stand in His holy place? He who has clean hands and a pure heart, who does not lift up his soul to an idol or swear by what is false. He will receive blessing from the Lord and vindication from God his Savior. Such is the generation of those who seek Him, who seek your face, O God of Jacob. Lift up your heads, O you gates; be lifted up, you ancient doors, that the King of glory may come in. Who is this King of glory? The Lord strong and mighty, the Lord mighty in battle. Lift up your heads, O you gates; lift them up, you ancient doors, that the King of glory may come in. Who is He, this King of glory? The Lord Almighty – He is the King of glory.

Zechariah 7:9 "This is what the Lord Almighty says: 'Administer true justice; show mercy and compassion to one another.' "

Zechariah 8:15-17 "... Do not be afraid. These are the things you are to do: Speak the truth to each other, and render true and sound judgment in your courts; do not plot evil against your neighbor, and do not love to swear falsely. I hate all this," declares the Lord.

My church must awake from slumber, stand for justice and confront deception and evil. You must not be afraid, but instead trust in Me - knowing that I will destroy the enemy.

Personal Revelation;

Divorce Baal. Period.

The Sanctuary of Pan

Day 34 Listen

1 Samuel 15:22-23 But Samuel replied: "Does the Lord delight in burnt offering and sacrifices as much as in obeying the voice of the Lord? To obey is better than sacrifice, and to heed is better than the fat of rams. For rebellion is like the sin of divination, and arrogance like the evil of idolatry. Because you rejected the word of the Lord, He has rejected you ..."

Micah 6:8 ... And what does the Lord require of you? To act justly and to love mercy and to walk humbly with your God.

Matthew 12:7-8 "If you had known that these words mean, 'I desire mercy, not sacrifice,' you would not have condemned the innocent. For the Son of Man is Lord of the Sabbath."

Personal Revelations;

Golan Heights (memorial) with Syria in the background

Day 35   Speak Forth

Mars Hill, location of Paul's speech of the Unknown God, Athens, Greece

Psalm 84:5-12 Blessed are those whose strength is in you, who have set their hearts on pilgrimage. As they pass through the Valley of Baca, they make it a place of springs; the autumn rains also cover it with pools. They go from strength to strength, till each appears before God in Zion. Hear my prayer, O Lord God Almighty; listen to me, O God of Jacob. Look upon our shield, O God; look with favor on your anointed one. Better is one day in your courts than a thousand elsewhere; I would rather be a doorkeeper in the house of my God than dwell in the tents of the wicked. For the Lord God is a sun and shield; the Lord bestows favor and honor; no good thing does He withhold from those who walk blameless. O Lord Almighty, blessed is the man who trusts in You.

Genesis 18:17-26 Then the Lord said, "Shall I hide from Abraham what I am about to do? Abraham will surely become a great and powerful nation, and all nations on earth will be blessed through him. For I have chosen him, so that he will direct his children and his household after him to keep the way of the Lord by doing what is right and just, so that the Lord will bring about for Abraham what he has promised him." ... Then Abraham approached him and said: "Will you sweep away the righteous with the wicked? ... Will not the judge of all the earth do right?" The Lord said, "If I find ... righteous people in the city ..., I will spare the whole place for their sake."

As the ancient ruins stand, so will you. As you speak forth the truth, there will be an eternal impact. The results will be life giving.

Personal Revelations;

Theatre of Beth Shean

Day 36 Submit

1 Samuel 15:1-29, 16:1-21 Samuel said to Saul, "I am the one the Lord sent to anoint you king over his people Israel; so listen now to the message from the Lord ... "I am grieved that I have made Saul King, because he has turned away from me and has not carried out my instructions." ... Samuel said, "... Why did you not obey the Lord? Why did you pounce on the plunder and do evil in the eyes of the Lord?" ... "Then Saul said to Samuel, "I have sinned. I violated the Lord's command and your instructions. I was afraid of the people and so I gave in to them." ... Samuel said to him, "... You have rejected the word of the Lord, and the Lord has rejected you as king over Israel!" As Samuel turned to leave, Saul caught hold of the hem of his robe, and it tore. Samuel said to him, "The Lord has torn the kingdom of Israel from you today and has given it to one of your neighbors – to one better than you. He who is the Glory of Israel does not lie or change his mind; for he is not a man, that he should change his mind." ... The Lord said to Samuel, "How long will you mourn for Saul, since I have rejected him as king over Israel? Fill your horn with oil and be on your way; I am sending you to Jesse of Bethlehem. I have chosen one of his sons to be king." ... "The Lord does not look at the things man looks at. Man looks at the outward appearance, but the Lord looks at the heart." ... So Samuel took the horn of oil and anointed him in the presence of his brothers, and from that day on the Spirit of the Lord came upon David in power. ... David came to Saul and entered his service ... David became one of his armor-bearers.

David loved his enemy more than himself – do you? *Really?*

Daniel 2:21 He sets up kings and deposes them

John 19:11 Jesus answered, "You would have no power over me if it were not given to you from above."

Romans 13:1 Everyone must submit himself to the governing authorities, for there is no authority except that which God has established. The authorities that exist have been established by God.

1 Peter 2:15-25 For it is God's will that by doing good you should silence the ignorant talk of foolish men ... show proper respect to everyone. Slaves, submit yourselves to your masters with all respect, not only to those who are good and considerate, but also to those who are harsh. For it is commendable if a man bears up under the pain of unjust suffering because he is conscious of God ... If you suffer for doing good and you endure it, this is commendable before God. To this you were called, because Christ suffered for you, leaving you an example, that you should follow in His steps. He committed no sin, and no deceit was found in His mouth. When they hurled their insults at Him, He did not retaliate; when He suffered, He made no threats. Instead, He entrusted himself to Him who judges justly. He Himself bore our sins in His body on the tree, so that we might die to sins and live for righteousness; by His wounds you have been healed. For you were like sheep going astray, but now you have returned to the Shepherd and overseer of your souls.

Personal Revelations;

Streets of Pillars leading off from Theatre - Beth Shean
(1 Samuel 31:10)

Day 37 Interdependency

1 Corinthians 12:1-30 Now about spiritual gifts, brothers, I do not want you to be ignorant. You know that when you were pagans, somehow or other you were influenced and led astray to mute idols. Therefore I tell you that no one who is speaking by the Spirit of God says, "Jesus be cursed," and no one can say, "Jesus is Lord," except by the Holy Spirit. There are different kinds of gifts, but the same Spirit. There are different kinds of service, but the same Lord. There are different kinds of working, but the same God works all of them in all men. Now to each one the manifestation of the Spirit is given for the common good. To one there is given through the Spirit the message of wisdom, to another the message of knowledge by means of the same Spirit, to another faith by the same Spirit, to another gifts of healing by that one Spirit, to another miraculous powers. To another prophecy, to another distinguishing between spirits, to another speaking in different kinds of tongues, and to still another the interpretation of tongues. All these are the work of one and the same Spirit, and He gives them to each one, just as He determines. The body is a unit, though it is made up of many parts; and though all its parts are many, they form one body. So it is with Christ. For we were all baptized by one Spirit into one body – whether Jews or Greeks, slave or free – and we were all given the one Spirit to drink. Now the body is not made up of one part but of many. If the foot should say, "Because I am not a hand, I do not belong to the body," it would not for that reason cease to be part of the body. And if the ear should say, "Because I am not an eye, I do not belong to the body," it would not for that reason cease to be part of the body. If the whole body were an eye, where would the sense of hearing be? If the whole body were an ear, where would the sense of smell be? But in fact God has arranged the parts in the body, every one of them, just as He wanted them to be. If they were all one part, where would the body be? As it is, there are many parts, but one body. The eye cannot say to the hand, "I don't need you!" And the head cannot say to the feet, "I don't need you!" On the contrary, those parts of the body that seem to be weaker are indispensable, and the parts that we think are less honorable we treat with special honor. And the parts that are unpresentable are treated with special modesty, while our presentable parts need no special treatment. But God has combined the members of the body and has given greater honor to the parts that lacked it, so that there should be no division in the body, but that its parts should have equal concern for each other. If one part suffers, every part suffers with it; if one part is honored, every part rejoices with it. Now you are the body of Christ, and each one of you is a part of it. And in the church God has appointed first of all apostles, second prophets, third teachers, then workers of miracles, also those having gifts of healing, those able to help others, those with gifts of administration, and those speaking in different kinds of tongues. Are all apostles? Are all prophets? Are all teachers? Do all work miracles? Do all have gifts of healing? Do all speak in tongues? Do all interpret? But eagerly desire the greater gifts. And now I will show you the most excellent way.

Since you're only a part, you can only see in part. If you're not obedient, you affect the entire body. You must answer the call without hesitation.

Personal Revelations;

Day 38   Stand

Isaiah 22:22-24 "I will place on his shoulder the key to the house of David; what he opens no one can shut, and what he shuts no one can open. I will drive him like a peg into a firm place; he will be a seat of honor for the house of his father. All the glory of his family will hang on him: its offspring and offshoots – all its lesser vessels, from the bowls to all the jars."

Joel 3:14-16 Multitudes, multitudes in the valley of decision! For the day of the Lord is near in the valley of decision. The sun and moon will be darkened, and the stars no longer shine. The Lord will roar from Zion and thunder from Jerusalem; the earth and the sky will tremble. But the Lord will be a refuge for His people, a stronghold for the people of Israel.

Zephaniah 3:9 "Then will I purify the lips of the peoples, that all of them may call on the name of the Lord and serve Him shoulder to shoulder."

Numbers 10:9-10 "When you go into battle in your own land against an enemy who is oppressing you, sound a blast on the trumpets. Then you will be remembered by the Lord your God and rescued from your enemies ... I am the Lord your God."

Psalm 20:6-9 Now I know that the Lord saves His anointed; He answers him from His holy heaven with the saving power of His right hand. Some trust in chariots and some in horses, but we trust in the name of the Lord our God. They are brought to their knees and fall, but we rise up and stand firm. O Lord, save the King! Answer us when we call!

Personal Revelations;

Caesarea

Call to battle - Valley of Armageddon

Day 39 Declare

1 Corinthians 14:8 Again, if the trumpet does not sound a clear call, who will get ready for battle?

Isaiah 42:9 "... and new things I declare; before they spring into being I announce them to you."

Personal Revelations;

Mount Carmel overlooking Armageddon

Day 40 Choice

Caesarea

Personal Revelations;

Mount Beatitudes

CPSIA information can be obtained
at www.ICGtesting.com
Printed in the USA
238089LV00001B

* 9 7 8 1 6 1 3 7 9 0 6 8 7 *